LOVE
LIFE
KINGDOM

LOVE, LIFE, KINGDOM

JULIAN VAUGHAN HAMPTON

"Love, Life, and Kingdom"
Written by Julian Vaughan Hampton
ISBN 0-9771160-1-8
ISBN 13- 9780977116010
LLCN- 2006925156
Published by VAUGHANWORKS,
P.O. Box 18511
Milwaukee, Wisconsin, 53218,
www.vaughanworks.com
vaughanworks1@mfire.com
1-877-829-6757

Manufactured in the United States

Table of Contents

Love

Life

Kingdom

Love, Life and Kingdom is a collection of poems reflecting on who we were, acknowledging who we are, and celebrating who we are destined to become. Each of us has a place deep within our hearts that yearns to be understood. These poems address those needs, tapping into the physical, emotional and spiritual position of the heart. Find the poems that draw you close to them, inspire you, or challenge your views of life. From joy to pain, success to failure, love lost and love gained, and finding your love and life within the kingdom.

I thank God for the liberty within my creativity.

Anything is Possible.
JVH

Fisherman

Fisherman, fisher of men

Casting my net unto the sea

Praying for strength to catch divine

A soul through prayer and testimony

Tumultuous tides that rock my vessel

Balance compromised in every way

Unfamiliar surroundings are self evident

A net that's tattered, torn, and frayed

A mission delivered from heaven itself

To work diligently, His word sublime

But winds of confusion toss wisdom aside

I find myself sinking an inch at a time

The more that I struggle, the deeper I fall

The more that I fight, the more I descend

And my disobedience prevents me from being

a true fisherman, a fisher of men

And though I lay on the ocean's floor

I call His name with both hands raised

He breathes His life into my lungs

Allowing me to sing His praise

And through the water he pulls me up

He dries me off and sets me straight

Commanding me to do His will

Demanding I cooperate

And once I say yes to His way

He pours new wine into my flask

He pours the word into my heart

For any questions one may ask

His guiding light, a beacon for souls

Vividly seen from distant glance

And that is where my calling lies

The place where my salvation stands

Fisherman, fisher of men

Casting my net into the sea

Praying for strength to catch divine

A soul through prayer and testimony

A KING FOR A QUEEN

My destination is in sight

I hope my decision is correct

For opportunities such as this

Come along once in a lifetime

I have journeyed far for this

Faced many perils, avoided many obstacles

The long, hard road has taken its toll on me

No chance for enduring another failure

This looks to be the grounds for my palace

I may yet be king

MAN OF GOD

A man of God, a world of sin

A restless soul that lies within

Spiritual rigamortis, I dare not die

A fear filled anointing, I must not cry

Still using a compass on a path that's

predestined

Still weighing all options when His will is

unquestioned

A man of God, a world of sin

Encouraged soul that lies within

A tainted heart, not completely clean

Yet strong belief in things unseen

A thirsting mind for word unknown

Union of saints and still unknown

Recognition I'm blessed beyond belief

Heaven above, the earth beneath

Among the latter and so I reach

With timid arms and stypheled speech

Too proud to learn, too humble to teach

Disobedient patience, a forced retreat

A man of God, a world of sin

A blessed soul that lies within

WOMAN OF GOD

Woman of God, a world denied

A nurturing soul that lies inside

Gift of creation, born to achieve

Body's a temple, beware of thieves

Trusting commitment, inspired dreams

Harbored resentment beneath the seams

Woman of God, a world denied

Inspired soul where faith resides

Instinctive will to overcome

A full day's struggle leaves night undone

Advising heart from experience gained

Prophetic gifts are self restrained

Woman of God, break through the chains

With willing praise and word ordained

Woman of God, no more denied

A blessed soul that dwells inside

IMAGES

I see it in your eyes

You are afraid of the future

You are regretting the past

Thinking of yourself as a failure

And it has halted your present

Wipe your eyes because life must go on

I can't say it will get any better

But just stay strong

And pray for the best

Then I left the mirror

LIGHT OF HOPE

There is only one light that gives me hope

All my companions have abandoned their
post

These same ones I would, as their mate,
give my life for

In this sea of life the tide turns so violently

Yet you stay to light the way for me

Only darkness and pain surround me

You are my one light

Without you I am lost

Please light my way

I THOUGHT I LOST MY PRAISE

One morning I rose from a slumber less
night

Had a frustrating week, and my soul wasn't
right

So I reached for my praise, but it stayed out
of sight

And I thought I lost my praise

Vain attempts to fulfill other's grandiose
views

Disregard for the season in which God says
to move

Leaving me paralyzed, hopeless and
confused

And I thought I lost my praise

Haunting memories unveil certain moments
of doubt

Overwhelmed by the fear of what could be
found out
Bringing wavering faith as the tears run
about

And I thought I lost my praise

I considered myself intellectually sound

Till the scope of my praise became
questioned abound

And the burden in my heart became so
profound

That I almost lost my praise

So I cried out to heaven and the one God I
know

And I asked where my praise went, which
way did it go

Was it taken away with the gifts you
bestowed?

Am I destined for hell and the dark world
below?

In my spiritual journey, have I traveled too
slow?

Have my tithes been too small or my
offerings too low?

Am I not yet forgiven for sins long ago?
Has my cup remained empty, free from
overflow?

I ask all these questions, and still I don't
know

And still I don't know, I don't know

So I asked for repentance for all of my sins

And I screamed the name Jesus again and
again

Started praying at 5 and I stopped around
10

And I still couldn't find my praise

I decided to praise just one final time

And that was the moment God sent me a
sign

Telling me he had heard me all of the time

And all of my forms of praise

He heard when I prayed, he heard when I
cried

He heard when I sang, or at least when I
tried

And one other thing that cannot be denied

I will never lose my praise

PERFECTION

If I were perfect, would you be happy

Because nothing would go wrong

If I were perfect, you'd have anything you wanted

And we'd always get along

But if I were perfect, it would be boring

Because I'd be too afraid

To laugh at imperfections

Or learn from mistakes that I made

If I were perfect, would you be happy

Because I'd never make you mad

But I'd be perfect, so you couldn't tell

My good points from my bad

Everyone wants that perfect mate

With this you may agree

But I wish you would love me for who I am

Because being perfect is not being me

IS IT LOVE

When eyes close, only your vision remains

A burning expectation in my heart

Not pain, not joy

Indescribable

Is it love?

Am I in love with you, or with love itself?

Still I want no other

Is it love?

THE BATTLE FOR MY SOUL

There I stood, a strong proud warrior

With the petulance of a young stallion

I assumed this day would be just another day that I vanquished an evil foe from my presence

Unfortunately, some spirits are stronger than expected

In my life's battlefield, I fought valiantly with the direction of my soul in the balance, yet victory slipped through my grasp

It was my own fault

The Father told me I could not prevail on my own, and he would assist me in my battles, but I was stubborn

He instructed me to guard his temple and keep the door shut tightly to prevent the enemy's entrance

To cover my ears and halt the exposure to his lies

To be aware of his trickery and his devious ways

I didn't listen, at least not well enough

The enemy remained outside the gate

A siren's call fell from a golden tongue

I became curious and cracked the open, only for an instance

I just wanted to see, I just wanted to know

That instance became infinitely more time than the enemy required

He was inside the temple, attempting to take residence

His sole purposes were to keep me from The Father's kingdom and to destroy me

He tried to comfort me, until I became uncomfortable with sin

He tried to entertain me, until I became bored with wrongdoing

I was tempted in complimented, while grace was preempted and evil was implemented

I thought he had robbed me of what he wanted, but he wanted more

He wanted my soul

He attacked, and the battle for my soul had begun

I moved against him, bible in hand in an arrogant attempt to dismantle the enemy with the double edged sword called the word

My lack of understanding led to the word slicing my own heart

Regrettably, I put my sword back into its sheath

My prayers inflicted damage on the evil ones, yet my own naivety proved to be a costly state

Wisdom danced around me, beckoning me with an unfamiliar tempo

My shield called faith gave a momentary barrier as I lay crouched beneath it

The attacks came again and again, nearly crushing my will to fight, my will to live

I began to wail; as my mouth expelled a language I myself had no comprehension of

I prayed for help and for strength, while my body weakened from the fight and my heart hardened

My soul searched for an escape
I cowered, humbled by my inability to handle the enemy

I glared upward from behind my shield

"I admit, I can't do it alone," I screamed

"Help me father," I screamed

Sliding backwards, I lost my footing

It was then that three most powerful allies came as one to my rescue

The first was The Father, glowing with a peacefully blinding light far too bright for my worldly eyes to see

He was all knowing and all powerful

He was the creator of all I knew and without Him I failed to exist

He cared enough to send his only Son to die for me

The second was His son named Jesus, possessing as bright a light as the Father, yet similar in some regards to me

He had a gloriously godly aura, but a connection with the common man

He was a protector, wise and true
My rescuer, with oils to heal wounds,
spiritual splints to set broken bones, and
the precious blood to cover me

A heavenly transfusion, replacing sin with
repentance for disobedience

He was willing to sacrifice himself for me,
and through him The Father addressed my
call

Finally, there was the Holy Spirit, which I
could not see, but felt his glory in my heart

As I praised the arrival, my strength grew,
and with it my will to fight, my will to live

When he fell upon me, I became renewed

When he filled me, I became whole

When he gave, I received

Together, the three fought as one

The battlefield moved to another realm

This was fought in a different dimension, an
expression of warfare, the governmental
prayer

I began to decree and declare to the
principalities that God move through the
nations, and He did move

The enemy I had struggled with just to keep
at bay was no match for my allies

The evil one circled around them, looking
for a way to attack me

He had no chance, for I had surrendered
my soul to the side of righteousness and an
all powerful alliance

The smoke cleared after my Lord conquered
the enemy, and I wiped my weary eyes

I could finally see the present day truth as I
stood on the cutting edge of the next world
order

I heard the clear and accurate voice of God,
and felt His hand on my shoulder

The enemy fled back into the shadows and
into the darkness

He would be back, if not to attack me, to
destroy another not protected

But this day I claimed victory
I would tell the land of my alliance with the
Lord, and the opportunity to claim one of
their own

A bond they themselves could lay claim to
The enemy was defeated before the next
battle was set to begin

I am victorious

MY GIFT

No need for a holiday

I give you this gift

Open it, you'll find my heart

I offer it to you with both hands

It is fragile, please take care of it

The longer you keep it

The stronger it becomes

But if by chance it is broken

It can never be as strong as it is now

It is an original, and can't be replaced

A gift, from me to you

SONGSCAPE

These notes, these lyrics, these rhythms
within this song create music, which is true

But they provide something containing
much more value

They provide a temporary escape

From the harsh realities of this world

There is no permanent escape

At least during this lifetime spent

So somehow this seems sufficient

For a time

So I rewind

And play it again

NUBIAN

No man can stand without a woman's hand

To guide him through his days

For this is known, let it be shown

Black women deserve our praise

Sweet as honey, strong as oak

Fertile as black soil

Talented and gifted, richer than any oil

From she who bore the man who later

Ruled a kingdom

To she that led a number of slaves
underground to freedom

To walk with the strut of a queen

While some show scorn to her face
Giving her one strike for her sex

Another strike for her race

This gives all the more reason

For us to stand and cheer

For all the black women who make it
through

The ones that persevere

FIRST AND SECOND STEPS

I've taken the first step toward love

It was a major task to uphold

As is the start of any goal

I am sure this is the proper path

I want to take

But is this the proper pace?

I have moved slowly to make

The journey as fulfilling as the end

But with this slow speed comes the fear

Of my goal moving away

I know the speed may throw me off track

But which chance will I take

Pull me up from this fallen state

I know there is another

Whom you must support

But if you save me

I shall prove myself worthwhile

My thanks is like no other

Ask yourself, and then decide

My next step depends on you

BEYOND REACH

The one thing I had longed for

Is out of my reach

I knew I could endure any situation

Knowing as long as there was a chance

My love for you would remain

As of now my lingering memory is of tears

Which only come when I feel strong enough

To show them

Hope for me is now a miracle

But don't miracles happen

Maybe

Maybe not this time

COMPOSITION FOR MY LOVE

Something is missing from my sentence

I need first to fill the vacant space

Then the full beauty of my line

Will be shown

I need not an ordinary word

But the one right word to fit my statement

So simple, yet so depressing

Have patience?

Patience is a virtue

But it is also a contradiction

The more patient I stay

The more impatient I get

My pen is to the pad once more

The due date is near

PANTHER

It wasn't me who stayed in the sun

Trying to reach the supple brownness of another

It wasn't my ancestors who frowned in disgust

Yet tried to rape a strong African mother

It wasn't my lips that smiled up close

Then spoke negatively when I walked away

It wasn't me that said "You people"

About something I did not do

I've never been a nigger

It relates to ignorance and I find strength in my race

While you stand jealous, frightened, paranoid

When the panther stalks the place

POWER

From the soulful realm of the mind deep within

Comes the power to impact, impart, and inspire mighty men

Those with their ear to The Lord, those who walk in their calling

Power

Like a bolt of lightning cast down from heaven, harnessed by a willing spirit

Reforming each and every environment you enter

Your footsteps are ordered by The Lord, stopping where your dominion lies

Destination Everywhere

Power

Sending shockwaves through the nations
Infinite aftershocks, reverberating through the community

Felt by all under God's reign

Power

Power to be both bold and humble
To master the marketplace

To allow The Lord to coordinate the agenda
of destiny

Power

Power to move toward confusion, conflict
and obstacles

Power to smash them into oblivion, yet
remain unchanged

To speak life or death

To heal and to forgive

To strategically achieve solutions and
results

Power

Power to be part of the foundation

Rarely seen, yet vital sound and reinforced

To be that which every structure relies
upon

Power

To be inspired, and fulfill The Lord's desire

Often challenged, frequently admired

To remember how much was given, and how much shall be required

Power

INDIVIDUAL FEELINGS

They say to have love, friendship must
come first

To appreciate the good times, you must live
through the worst

But if I care for you more than a friend
could

And all the times are lovely, isn't that just
as good?

They say you will know when the right
person's there

And the least likely couples will make the
best pair

But we have so much in common, and I
don't feel that way

Cause our love's like no other

So tell me

Who are they?

HOLDING HANDS

As we walk hand in hand

Each of your fingers are intertwined with
mine

Strengthening like links of a chain

Forged with our friendship

It foreshadows a love

Mutually shown and met halfway

Where our hands are bonded

This bond must be broken

But upon restoration, trust is found

And our relationship is strengthened

GOODBYE FRIEND

They call themselves friends and say that
they care, but I am not so sure

For friends don't add pain when the pain is
already too much to endure

They show you a side with love and comfort

That makes you long to be close

Which leaves you open with your guard
down

Because they know what hurts you the
most

These are not friends,

Yet neither am I if I continue to condemn
them

I am north and you are south

Your love or my forgiveness will lead us in
the same direction

Unlikely

I guess this is goodbye

RESOLUTION

As I plan my resolution

Its hard too understand

Why the things you want to change never

Turn out the way you've planned

You start out with a smile

This soon turns to a frown

As the months slowly roll by

And the trials of life get you down

But this year will be different

Much different than the last

For I have gained so much knowledge

From my troubles in the past

I set my goals carefully

Not too big or too small

And take each one step by step

So I'll achieve them all

Review them month by month

To see where I am at

And at the end I hope that when

I finally look back

I'll commend myself and give God thanks

For his great contribution

In helping me fulfill my dreams

My New Year's resolution

GRACE THROUGH THE FIRE

I step forward, facing a wall of fire

Too high to see over, beneath the surface
preventing me from seeing under

Too hot to get close enough to see through

My reflection flickering in the flames

Reminding me of my past failures

Things I found disappointing

My broken promises, hidden gifts and self
suppressed anointing

At a certain distance, that fire gave
comforting warmth

Allowing me excuses for my procrastination

But as I continue to step forward, my
comfort turns to pain

As the fire singes my spirit for a nano-
second

A moment in time marked by a
measurement like that (snap)

How long is that time?

It's as quick as the changing of the mind

As quick as the changing of the mind

As quick as it takes a man in darkness to recognize he is in darkness because he is blind

As quick as it takes to recognize a dream is more than a dream

It's a prophetic sign

I step away from the fire, turning and looking back for a safer pathway

Where the burdens weren't so heavy and the expectations weren't so high

Celebrating the taste of old wine

I found that pathway led to reliving the same challenges that were already a distant memory, already overcome

However, I can't turn back now

I won't turn back now

If moving forward leads to the leads to the ceasing of my existence, let me dance with the angels of heaven

But God had another agenda

Like a cloud signifying the approach of rain
A cloud signified the approach of the one
who reigns

And then came grace

Grace came like a cloak of protection

Tailored to perfection

Appropriate for all seasons

Complimenting my kingdom ensemble

And it made me look good

That grace covered every aspect of my
personal I was ashamed to reveal

The fire raised its flames, anticipating my
demise

But with grace I walked boldly through it

Not a hair on my head changed
temperature

Not even a degree

I met glory on the other side and gave it to
My Lord

Not even a fraction of the competent
amount he deserves, but glory nonetheless

ONE VIEW

As you take this picture of me

Keep every aspect as it is

There is no need to erase prior lines

Or draw new ones

If you care for the picture

Why try to see it differently

Other's views are secondary

Take them as so

I am true

ON THE INSIDE

One after another, I feel them fall

With each one I learn a new lesson

Sometimes they come for reasons unknown

Only my heart knows, but it won't tell

It has gone through so much pain already

What makes it so bad is that

They lie within

And I haven't the courage to retrieve them

DREAM LOVER

You've had a rough day

Close your eyes, let dreams be your guide

I'll be there to make sure your needs are
fulfilled

For your dreams are my dreams

Your wishes, mine as well

Let your imagination run wild

I am your hero, your lover, your servant

And the mood is always right in our dreams

If you fall, I will catch you

Save you from any danger

No rescue is too perilous for me

Your dream lover

And when you awake, I'll be there

To do the same

Good morning

I hope you slept well

SAHARA

A desert sits in common with our
relationship

They're both so dry and empty

Ever so desolate

I'm tired of going through both of them
blindly

And with it the wild winds that blow

When all it will take is a little love in them

To make beautiful things grow

Yet just like a cactus, you're stubborn

And don't wish to bloom with good things

It's the fact that I still care, which hurts

More than a scorpion's sting

So now I know it's over

Because you refuse to try

While people circle like vultures

Waiting for our love to die

INTENSITY

Such a distance apart

Yet just out of reach

A bond, strong when we're together

More true when we are apart

Thirst for what I longed for is quenched

Expressible through neither word

Nor speech

Holding more love

Than an envelope can carry

Relationship

More powerful than I ever conceived

Present

Everyday a holiday

Away

Loyalty without doubt

EXACT

There is only one center on a bull's eye

Every other circle surrounding the core

Is missing the mark

When the spiritual crosshairs are aligned

And the apostolic target is in range

I decree we will make contact

Close is missing

Near is not close enough

To the core, the center, the epicenter

The focal point

When the puzzle of life has a missing piece

There is one exact piece that turns a part
into a whole

A fragment into a picture

If it's not exact, the piece won't fit

Even if the piece is forced into place

It is never really in place
Exact is a point of contact

A place of impact

A place called there

A time called now

Not now and then, now and when

Apostolic and prophetic

The present and the future, simultaneously

Thy kingdom come, Thy will be done
In earth as it is in heaven

Exact is a map with a clearly defined
destination

Peripheral wilderness is merely a landmark

We move past the distractions and step
forward with focus

Determined to finish

Expectations of overflow are done

With balance

The trinity, a triangle that if turned upside
down must be balanced exactly on its point

to be in proper position to achieve
maximum stability
An exact measurement is necessary

For the fullness of any vessel

Any less is incomplete

Exact is decree and done

Declare and done

An instantaneous manifestation

It takes exact notes to create a harmony

Out of key is noise

Not natural, but spiritual

We harmonize with clarity

No interference or static in our station

In designing the kingdom

The design must be followed exactly

Missing a brick or a beam

Could be devastating, signifying collapse

Never underestimate your cornerstone

The foundation is laid

Shifting only when it is time to shift
Never before or after

Exact is a cohesive community

An exact replica of the kingdom of God

Never settling for adequate

But planning for excellence

Exact order

Not just decreeing, but declaring the decree

A better covenant

Done in a more excellent way

A changed heart and reformed

A changed mind and reformed

A more excellent desire for the more
excellent provider, Jehovah Jira

The design by the designer

The refiner

The one who sent his only son as a
constant reminder

Exact is the conformity of the nations

With the word of God written in your heart
And no room for misinterpretation

Downloads and getting a hit

With prayers in a constant state of
transition

Speaking to God and getting a response

Exact is 10 being the number of the law

There could not be 11 commandments

The arc had to be constructed to exact
specifications with the exact numbers of
beings within

Any less would lead to the failure to
replenish the earth

I could go on and on

But the point is in designing kingdom
communities for the 21st century and
beyond

We must move past accurate into exactness
To achieve the will of God

TO OVERCOME

My heart beat disturbingly fast

Sweat streamed down my brow

Trickling near my left eye

Squinting to avoid the burning

Hands trembling, lungs searching for air

Heart for inspiration

Mind for confidence

Body for composure

Asking myself, "What are you doing?

Men have trained all their lives to be good at this."

Struggling, reminding myself to just put one foot in front of the other

I wasn't far

I felt a world away

Mouth too parched to swallow

Can't anyway, with this lump in my throat

Prematurely exhausted

Doubt negating my swagger

My competition has their second wind

A sip of water

A long inhale

A longer exhale

And I asked the beauty her name

THE KEYHOLE

The keyhole

A portal to a land of happiness and love

If only we were small enough to enter

And pass through the other side

We may only peer through

And long for what is on the other side

But never enter

So what use is it?

But for a key

AN EMPTY CLOSET

My closet is my heart

It is closed from within

If I were to open it

Emptiness I would find

I know not who holds the key

To which this lock binds

It is them whom I search for

To set my heart free

It is sensitive

If opened with force it would break easily

The scars on the oak

Tell the pain my heart has felt

There are the grains which show

Life still exists

Curiosity is tempting

So I cannot resist

Looking for someone to blame for the crime

I find I have been holding the key

All the time

A LESSON IN ABSENCE

In the fall

The leaves turn a beautiful array of colors

It seems as if they know winter is coming

And try to make their last days memorable

The leaves fall

And soon the cold, lonely frost comes

Yet the trunk stays strong

Every limb depends on its existence

Soon the frost melts

And even the saddest willow blossoms

The magnificent leaves return

And the beauty is even more fulfilling

Since the trunk was strong

During the absence

SHIELD TO THE HEART

It is night, alone I walk

A tear streaks from my eye

Remembrance of our past

Of days gone by

When you wanted more than friendship

And I told you we should wait

Leaving my heart open

Trying to keep your feelings safe

Now the blow has struck me harshly

This pain I cannot bear

You seem to want another with a love

That cannot be shared

And now I must retreat

For my fight was to no avail

The thought of another ship has taken

The wind out of my sails

So now I sit alone

With only a memory to embrace

Trying to hide the pain

That is written on my face

I wouldn't call it love

But it must be something near

And if it is indeed love

I shield it due to fear

So if you do care for me

Now is the time to say

Because soon I may be gone

Although my love will always stay

PINE

There I stood

Planted in the lawn in front of your house

I waited for you, and like clockwork

You came home from work

At 5:45 you pulled in the driveway as usual

In your navy blue eighties model sedan

The brakes you procrastinate about getting fixed squealed louder than normal

You turned on your favorite Aero smith song

Loosened your tie, and just sat there

I saw that look in your eyes

I know it well

It was that 'somebody just pissed me off' look

You opened the door and stepped out

Wearing that tacky, clearance rack blazer

Those wrinkled brown slacks were a size too small

And those loafers curled at the tip

You slammed the door

Mumbling something under your breath

"What a jerk," I thought to myself

After fidgeting with your keys

You entered the house

I glared through the large glass window

When you tossed your fake leather briefcase on the cream colored love seat

I watched her lovingly walk toward you in an obvious attempt to show your affection

You frowned at her

You screamed at her

Called her every name in the book

Then you hit her

I saw it, you pathetic bastard

She is the mother of your child

How could you hit her?

Or any woman, for that matter

I made as much noise as I could

But no one was listening

I wish I could beat the hell out of you

Or defend her

Show you how to treat a woman

But I can't

For I am just a tree

And we just don't do that

So you closed the window

And continued

SHADOW

He is there

When I turn on the light

He stays by my side

Faithful and true

As I wake in the morn

He guards me

When there is trouble and no one will stay

He remains

The lone figure on this earth

I dare say I trust

Compatible

Like myself in every active aspect

But when I'm in darkness

Who do I turn to?

ADVICE

For so long I have wandered

Trusting no one in my path

Thinking everyone who entered my future

Was no better than those in my past

But the love of a caring friend changed that

And I knew that she was right

When she told me you have to trust someone

Sometime in your life

So I searched within myself

Within my heart and mind

And found what I'd been searching for

Was right there all the time

Now I reach to her

But she's now willing to take my hand

She has doubts about our future

So I sit on desolate land

She told me I should take a chance

Why won't she do the same?

When so little could be lost

But so much could be gained

If only someone who is so wise

Could learn to take their own advice

MAY I

May I show you the moon?

With just enough light

To appreciate love's beauty

Yet keep the moment intimate

May I show you the sun?

With just enough warmth

To keep our love heated

When in each other's arms

May I show you the stars?

With just enough brightness

For us to make wishes

For undying love

I would show you the universe

If I only could

If you just lay by my side

We can truly see all

And not leave the comfort

Of each other's arms

ON YOU

It is now getting late

I sit alone and I contemplate

How I can get to know you better

I hesitate

Because I would hate to be rejected

So I protected

My heart's a shield that I wield

A new perspective

That I think of you

Night and day I do

The feelings I hold inside have grown to

Enormous proportions

Love without distortion

Our future's clear, all I see is fortune

For us and the life we lead

It's you that I need

In this garden of love

I'll plant the first seed

But it's up to you to provide the sunlight

If we ever want to take our love

To new heights

Am I right?

Tell me if I ain't

A beautiful picture

I hold in my hand the paint

Take the brush if you feel the same as me

Go for broke, one stroke

You'll have a masterpiece

SCREENPLAY

From the moment I opened my eyes

To a sky where the sun did not shine

I knew deep down inside

Today would not be mine

Stepping from a state of mind

Deeper than the deepest abyss

Hit with the unyielding force of reality

Bringing memories of what

I most dearly miss

In my mind lies a universe

Filled with dimensions

Most couldn't dare comprehend

It is distorted

And realistically, it's foolish to pretend

That optimism is here

I am no actor, this is no play

For on this day I need more

Than a director to direct my way

Because no matter how tall

No matter how wide

No screen could fully capture

Just what I feel inside

STRENGTH WITHIN WEAKNESS

Is it wrong to have a warm heart?

The softness and intense emotions that flourish within it can be a blessing

But it seems to be a curse in times like these

Cursed with a weakness

That cannot be strengthened

I search for a new weapon

Strong enough to defend my weakness

There is pride, morality, and honor

But combine these three and they still don't equal the strength of love

No mater how I try

My love burns through this shield of hate

Maybe my love is in fact a powerful weapon

My greatest weakness is also my most powerful weapon

Is this possible?

TO A DYING RELATIONSHIP

One day I picked a flower

A beautiful gold flower

With fragrance above all others

As I cared for it, it blossomed

For it was nurtured

As there is spring, there is also winter

And through these times

The sun did not shine as brightly

I told my flower, "If you make it through these times, a joyous time awaits you and your petals will stretch to the sun. I will do everything in my power to help, and to keep you strong."

My flower gave up the will to fight

And soon died

Now my window pane is bare

With only a vase to remind me of my flower

A TASTE OF HEAVEN

She must appear

But when, where, how

This love of mine

Whom I have waited infinite eternities

But still have not found

My queen

With whom I will build a kingdom

On this place we call earth

Will she be sent through a portal

Into my anticipating arms

Or will she come when I am old and gray

And content is the only life I'd know

So I'd care less

Will my heat erupt in joy

To tell me this is her

Or will I fail to believe that she is the one

And let her pass by

Whenever, wherever, however she comes

It doesn't matter

As long as she is the one

I may receive my taste of heaven

Ahead of time

REMNANT

The stars remind me of you

And the fact that someday my wish

May come true

The sunrise reminds me of you

It gives me just another day

To show how much I care for you

The night reminds me of you

As I kneel to give thanks

For your friendship

The spring reminds me of you

The way things grow

And so will we

The fall reminds me of you

And those deep, romantic brown eyes

I lose myself each time I see you

The falling rain reminds me of you

My heart beats with each falling drop

You provide me with the sunlight

Even on those darkest nights

While the taste of your sweet lips

Send electricity through my body

The winter reminds me of you

And how cold I am when you're not around

The summer reminds me of you

The heat and intensity we create

When we're together

FROM VICTIM TO TORMENTOR

My lesson has been learned well

It has taken many teachers

To know the truth

Although experience is in fact

The best teacher

I learned the hard way

I shall never forget my lesson

Nor shall I forget my teachers

For someday I shall be the one

Teaching what I have learned

As hard as it was taught to me

Revenge, possibly

More likely to ease the pain

Time cannot cure

Wrong, definitely

It is far easier being the tormentor

Than to be the victim

CALENDAR

Days have become months

Months have become years

Yet these visions grasp the deepest

Reaches of my mind

A touch of hope lies dormant

In my every dream

Which gives reality less worth that it seems

I pray it be just a matter of time

Far too many stars have been wished upon

Far too many times have I lay to rest

Far too many nights have I awaken

From the darkness

To the loud, empty sounds of loneliness

If time moved counter clockwise

But only for a day

One could utilize the things they do

Or change the things that one might say

But in reality it is a fact

Time will never take a step back

For destiny I must find another way

So I turn the final page of my calendar

And concentrate on the days yet to come

FAIRYTALE

He is your night in shining armor

With all the worldly possessions

You could imagine

Beautiful is his castle

You could bathe in his gold

Dry yourself with the finest silk

He is well schooled

His intelligence is unrivaled

Every word is spoken in a royal tongue

He could show you the world if you desired

But is that enough?

I am but a peasant

I don't have much to give

But I would share all I possess with you

I have no castle

But the kingdom in my heart

In which you already dwell

You could bathe in my love

Dry yourself in my arms

Which give more warmth than any silk

My tongue is not royal

But my words are truthful

They can clearly express any love

My heart holds

I can't show you the world

But together we can make dreams to places

Beyond the realm of a map

For love has no boundaries

My princess

You deserve the best

Whatever the best may be to you

Someday I may be a prince

But if not, when material things are gone

It matters most what is underneath

So I present myself to you

Heart and soul

But is that enough?

MM YEAH

Think about that someone

That special someone

Who does that something

You know that one thing

That makes your heart quiver

Spine shiver, when the deliver

A sliver of emotion, a quotient so fine

It penetrates the deepest reaches of your

Mind, body and soul, united

A complex equation

Me plus you equals elation

Me plus you equals celebration

Me plus you equal anticipation

Me plus you, me plus you, me plus you

I'm trying to get back on track

But the more I say it, the more I love it

The more I think it, the more I love you

Man, I like the sound of that

I hope you don't mind if I read it back

I could say that forever

And the day after that

Me plus you

Because when it comes to our love

It's a complex equation

Me plus you equals elation

Me plus you equals celebration

Me plus you equals anticipation

Spiritual compensation

A sensual collaboration

An emotional consummation

Then the equation moves to another level

Of complication

When in this situation

I am the addend X

And you are the addend y

And every imaginable sum is love

Now if you take that number

And multiply it by pi

That approximately 3.14 hours a day

I have the pleasure of your company

The only variable is time

My time, your time, our time

The more time we share

The more love is there

Any fraction or subtraction

Would be a distraction

For my love only deals with whole numbers

And we move past the negatives

Dwelling in the positives

And I'm positively into you

All I can say is MM Yeah

Think about that true love

That I do love

That I'm willing to do whatever it takes

To pursue love

That I don't care what anybody else

In the world thinks about you love

Its all about you love

That first sight love

That just right love

That all I want to do is be with you tonight

Love

That I swear if anybody messes with you

I'm down to fight love

That let me give you a massage

Because you look a little uptight

Love

The in the middle of my darkest moments

You are my guiding light, love

That calm, cool comforting

Everything is gonna be alright

Love

That I could see your beauty

Even if I lost my sight, love

That if loving you is wrong

I don't wanna be right, love

That I love you despite, love

That I'll love you all night love

That top notch butterscotch caramel delight

Love

That

That

That

I guess what I'm trying to say is

I love you

Plain and simple

I love you
All I can say is MM Yeah

GLOOM

Some days the clouds are out

As is the case today

There are too many of them

For the sun to break through

It has been raining for so long

Everything is so gray and dismal

The fog is thick

And covers all

When will it stop?

WHAT ARE YOU SEARCHING FOR

What is it you are searching for?

Ask yourself

You are traveling a treacherous road

Looking for a place to settle

Somewhere you will feel safe as a baby

In its mother's arms

Where you will feel warmth

As if the sun itself gently caressed you

Your first steps were filled with hurt

Pain and frustrations

The raindrops of discontent poured

Upon your every being

So you left

Now you walk through a camp

Where you are most welcome

Where you are thought of as a queen

Where you may settle down

And call this place your own

Knowing this

Why would you take another step?

Do you find it better to continue down

A perilous road

Than to stop where it may be safe?

Clouds may lie ahead of you

And in front of you

But there are clear skies right above you

GREED

I want it

Call me selfish, but it is so tempting

I dream of it every night

But observe it from a distance

For it belongs to another

Who takes good care of it

Not letting it out of sight

But now that I've seen it

I will always want it

Someday I will have it

LONG WALK

This is such a barren and lonely road

I have been traveling for a long time now

Frustration shows, as I wipe my eyes

My hope, blown away like the sands

Surrounding me

I hunger

So many have passed

But none have shown me refuge

So I continue walking

THOUGHTS OF A TROUBLED RECRUIT

They told me to take it in stride

As my family cried

When the mailman came to the door

Telling me I had been drafted for war

In a foreign land, against my own will

To fight for a country that didn't care

About me until it was time

To cross the enemy's boundary line

A sentence of death

I didn't even commit a crime

Nothing to do but to count the days

And pray something happens

So they won't send me away

I should have listened to my own intuition

Found revelation I had made the wrong
decision

My mind was focused on my future
ambition

Joined the institution for tuition assistance

But before I knew it, it was time to depart

With twenty other brothers all with the
same fear in their heart

Each one wondering what type of horror
was intact

In a place they only knew from a map

Called Iraq

But my state of my changed when the plane
lands

It was 120 degrees in the shadow of the
desert sand

As they assign me for more of this tour

It's hard to endure

I'm not even sure what we're fighting this
war for

I ask myself day to day

Is it for oil, for peace, for revenge, for
freedom, for pride, or for this idea called the
American way?
They take me out of my daily routine

Turn me into a killing machine

And then give me a medal when I kill
another human being

But many have fought so that I may fight

So many have broken through daily
bondage so that I am able to rest in a free
nation at night

And I offered my life to defend other's rights

Plus, what's done in the darkness shall be
revealed in the light

So if I don't move, then who will?

And who's gonna move if I choose to stay
still?

Because my cross and my gun are both
made of the same steel

One symbolizes eternal life

The other is forged to kill

So many dreams in my life yet to fulfill are
merely footnotes when I'm writing my will

It will be no surprise if death is my fate

If I wait to see the whites of their eyes

It'll be too late

In a bed of bloodshed, my enemy and I may lay together

I put faith in the possibility that someday our children will play and pray together

So if my casket is covered with a flag representing the country I love

And the fighter jets stream through the air just above

Let me legacy ensure my family's loss would be the next generation's gain

And know that I had a dream, a purpose, a calling, and an anointing

I gave my life for you

I was not just another soldier slain

One nation, under God, indivisible

With liberty and justice for all

THE DAWN'S CHILL

As the dawn approaches

No warmth has come with the rising sun

Chills are sent through a warm body

And an ever warmer heart

But the crisp, cold air is nothing

Compared to the chill of a man

That has given up hope

Many mornings have a awaken to the sun

It produced the possibilities of a bright
future through the perils of the present

But this has been a different morning

There is nothing in sight but the pale flakes

A sign of emptiness

I look to the one space in the clouds for
inspiration

But it is soon overcome by gray

I try to look within myself
But I no longer have the strength

Or the will

Now I know I must look past the snow

Past the clouds, to the heavens

Because that is the only way hope may
return to one that has spent

Too long in the cold

THE ABYSS

What do you do when you've come to a
point where you can't take it anymore?

When you've tried your hardest

Yet words of encouragement are little more

Than mere phrases with little meaning

When you realize nothing is all you have

And every day emphasizes that fact

When those you hold dearest are the ones
furthest from your reach

When your mind is an abyss filled with
sunken hopes and dreams

When your heart is but a target aimed at
one too many times

When your body is tired from carrying the
pressure that the mind and heart can't bear

When trust is something that never was

Love something that may never be

And faith is the only link to the memory of
the two
Again I ask

What do you do?

You pray

KINGDOM MAN

Being a Kingdom Man means being a man of the kingdom

Having the ability to be transformed like Paul

The courage of David, The wisdom of Solomon, the technology of Noah,

The love of Jesus, and if that's not all

To have the relationship of Adam with God, before the fall

Consistently matching internal and external

God's fire burning inside you, a Kingdom infernal

Moving from old things the mind embraces

For accuracy to exactness, and hitting those thin places

All with the expectation that God's will be fulfilled

No longer focusing on the blessing, but celebrating the build

Your sons will surpass you, your daughters will too

They will never be able to comprehend the
struggles you knew

They'll tap into the wealth of wisdom you've
amassed

The prophetic words spoken over their lives

Will all come to pass

They'll possess the land, they'll take their
dominion

And pay no mind to the enemy's opinion

Because you have the victory

Why because you're not alone

Let's look at it in another way

Let me delve deeper

Because this one's a keeper

If three fingers represent three, the number for
the trinity

And two fingers are the symbols that means
victory

Then one finger by itself is merely an obscenity

And we are to kingdom for that

So we move from singular to corporate

We are a community

And the only one that matters is God

From me's to we's

From I's to us

From church to kingdom

Fulfilling God's purpose

We do what we do, an apostolic mouthpiece

We use what procedeth from the mouth of God through us

To spread reformation from the Northwest to the Southeast

Keep teaching apostolic principles, walk eternal not temporal

For in these days, a kingdom man's role is so pivotal

From spirit led to spiritual

From analog to digital

Demystifying the prophetic, so it's no longer mystical

Break through anything that is causing resistance

I speak breakthrough in the atmosphere

And call it into existence

From books, conferences, and spoken word cds

To radio, talk shows, and ministry tv

To things that have never been witnessed before

With open ears to hear the lion of Judah's roar

All with the purpose of the kingdom in mind

Searching for deep things, rejoicing the find

There's something inside just waiting for birthing

Living waters are flowing and the nations are thirsting

For a man of the kingdom that will finally take a stand

And live out his calling as a true kingdom man

BLACKNESS

It wasn't all that long ago

When the people from the continent of
Africa were the original

Makers and builders of this earth

And for what it's worth

It was a gift instilled in blacks from birth

Because we were first

But our people were taken from their homes
for duration

Put on plantations in a foreign nation

Introduced to terms like slavery and
segregation

Destroying the hope of the next generation

The land of the free, the home of the brave

Where African kings and queens were made
house slaves

They found that they could keep blacks down

If the kept us ignorant of our background

They changed our description from a kingly adjective

Into a degrading pronoun

Took away our tribal drums in an attempt to extinguish the sound

Interrupted our dialect and changed our environment

Prepared us for extinction or a spiritual retirement

They knew blacks couldn't feel superior

If they stripped away our dominant interior

And continued to teach us our people were inferior

But a few knew that this was just not true

All they needed was a clue for what to do

There was a higher agenda for us to pursue

As we eliminated the false and bathe in the new

So embrace this concept as we mentally
hold hands

And like Martin Luther King, we'll find the
promised land

Strength, power, dominion, blackness

Authority, priority, majority, blackness

Creative, innovative, demonstrative,
blackness

Strength, power, dominion, blackness

The colors representing the continent of
Africa

The red, black and green are the colors in
fact

It does get much deeper than that

There's the red that stands for the
bloodshed

Those who gave their lives so that we can
get ahead

For those whose souls cry out from the
dead

We neglect knowledge of our history, while
American history is force fed

The black is for the people the land holds

Because there we built kingdoms

And here we built railroads

Under the master's whip

Blacks worked until the dropped

And if they tried to escape they were
stopped

By a gunshot for defying command

Which brings us to the green that stands
for the land

United we fall, together we stand

Believing through our faith, we overcome
and

In our blackness, we shall survive

We thrive, preparing for what lies on the
other side

As who we are fades, who we will become
starts to rise

And like Jesse Jackson said

We keep hope alive

Strength, power, dominion, blackness

Authority, priority, majority, blackness

Creative, innovative, demonstrative, blackness

Strength, power, dominion, blackness

Black pride, we must let it spread worldwide and contininental

Knowledge is the key to our community, its essential

To reach our full potential

The youth must find the proof

And move past any dissention

Concentrating on the creativity

Knowledge of our forefather's inventions

From the air conditioner, invented by Fredrick M Jones

To Henry T Sampson, who invented the
cellular phone

Alexander Miles created the elevator

WA Martin invented the lock

J Standard invented the refrigerator

Paul L Downing invented the mailbox

From baby buggies, dust pans, and the
auto cut off switch

To the clothes dryer, pencil sharpener, and
automatic gear shift

From the tricycle, the stove, and spark
plugs for your car

To traffic lights, rolling pins, lawn mowers
and guitars

All inventions from blacks, just to name a
few

The next space on the list is just waiting for
you

So search deep within, it's a constant
pursuit

While black history is being written, what
will you contribute?

Blank pages await you, your ideas and your thoughts

The obstacles you've faced and the battles you fought

A legacy left for a day yet to come

When black kings and queens return to their kingdoms

Strength, power, dominion, blackness

Authority, priority, majority, blackness

Creative, innovative, demonstrative, blackness

Strength, power, dominion, blackness

IS LOVE GOOD OR BAD

Love is a terrifying thing

It forces you to open up every internal
aspect of yourself

Every skeleton, every discrepancy,
everything

It is remorseful, forgiving, intense,
unpredictable, humble, and tolerant

It is a paper thin glass, on which a
foundation is laid

It is an empire, when fully constructed
becomes a stronghold nothing can destroy

It is a double edged sword, a treacherous
hike, and immeasurable celebration

An unbreakable bond, united and true

Love guarantees nothing, but risks
everything

It is a rhetorical question; a heart felt
soliloquy rarely said, continuously felt

A conversation between two souls saying
yes I do, I do too

It is an emotional ballet, choreographed to
perfection

A life vest, unsolved riddle needing only to
be addressed, but not deciphered

It is a diamond necklace, impressive
without flamboyance, or a piece of rope
given with sincerity, even more valuable

UNTIL NOW

Never had I realized important you were to me, until now

Never had I wondered how it would be if you were gone, until now

Its not that I took you for granted

Or that I couldn't live without you

But I never missed someone so much, until now

Seems like just yesterday we were planning our future

Thinking nothing could go wrong

So I assumed our love was strong

Until now

But for today, you've gone away

And I think about what could have been

Things I could have done different then

And wondered if I should try again

Until now

IF I DIED

If I died right now, could I honestly say

That I'd done enough to deserve his grace

In his heavenly palace, have I earned a place?

I just can't say for sure

If my answer to the question is anything but yes

A vague assumption, a scientific guess

It doesn't matter my opinion or fleshly analysis

It just means I need to do more

If right at this moment my last breath was spent

In my heart of all hearts would I be content

In knowing He accepted my chance to repent

I pray that it be true

For the clock called my life is not set by me

It's determined by Thee, The Divine Trinity

Standing at heaven's gate with the spiritual key

I pray I'm prepared to use

WHO DO I PRAY FOR

In this time of turbulence within our land

No one to believe in, by faith we stand

And love ones lost, knocking on heaven's door

One question remains, who do I pray for

For my country, who retaliates to preserve my freedom, but only find it appropriate to profess their faith in God in times of turmoil? God bless America

For those near and far who wish to kill my family, my friends, and myself for reasons beyond my understanding?

How do you kill in the name of God?

For my fatigued grabbed neighbor, who waves nonchalantly, and could be called to risk his life and limb to defend this country?

For the group of protestors on the local news? They cry for peace until their family is victimized.

For those discriminated against because of
their similar culture, and despite their
dissimilar beliefs?

For myself, feeling hopeless beyond the
power of prayer and donations?

For the deceased, the injured, the lost, and
their loved ones?

I pray for them all, because God wants it
that way.

QUICK ORDER FORM

"Love, Life and Kingdom"
List price $12.95

Website: www.vaughanworks.com

Email orders- vaughanworks1@mfire.com

Telephone Orders- Call 1-877-VAWORKS (829-6757) toll free.

Postal Orders- VAUGHANWORKS
C/O Julian Vaughan Hampton
PO Box 18511-0511
Milwaukee, WI 53218, USA

Shipping by air-

U.S.: Please add $3.00 for the first book and $2.00 for each additional product.
International: Please add $6.00 for the first book, and $4.00 for each additional book (estimate).

For speaking engagements, seminars, interviews, or any of the Vaughanworks services, call, email, or mail request to the addresses listed above.

Printed in the United States
53715LVS00002B/28-75